Gift Exchange

Margo Klundt

Trilogy Christian Publishers
A Wholly Owned Subsidiary of Trinity Broadcasting Network
2442 Michelle Drive
Tustin, CA 92780

Copyright © 2023 by Margo Klundt

Unless otherwise indicated, scripture quotations are taken from the King James Version of the Bible. Public domain.

All rights reserved, including the right to reproduce this book or portions thereof in any form whatsoever.

For information, address Trilogy Christian Publishing
Rights Department, 2442 Michelle Drive, Tustin, CA 92780.
Trilogy Christian Publishing/ TBN and colophon are trademarks of Trinity Broadcasting Network.

For information about special discounts for bulk purchases, please contact Trilogy Christian Publishing.

Trilogy Disclaimer: The views and content expressed in this book are those of the author and may not necessarily reflect the views and doctrine of Trilogy Christian Publishing or the Trinity Broadcasting Network.

10 9 8 7 6 5 4 3 2 1

Library of Congress Cataloging-in-Publication Data is available.

ISBN 979-8-89041-442-7
ISBN 979-8-89041-443-4 (ebook)

Acknowledgements

Linda Tuthill: Thank you for asking me to participate in the Christmas program. This book would not have been written otherwise.

Ellen Miller and Melvin Klundt: Thanks for your encouragement through the writing of the story.

Our Father in heaven: Most of my praise and thanks goes to You for the story inspiration, for leading me to the "behind the scenes" hidden gems of the nativity story, and then for encouraging me to submit the story for others to read. I felt a little like the lamb in the story, being nudged along by Your staff and loving hands.

The night was calm and clear, and the stars were twinkling brightly against the black velvet sky. Especially visible was an unusually big, bright star. I was resting with the others in the fields near Bethlehem.

Suddenly, the silence was broken, and we were stunned and surrounded by the brilliance of an angel who said:

"Fear not: for, behold, I bring you good tidings of great joy, which shall be to all people. For unto you is born this day in the City of David a Savior, which is Christ the Lord. And this shall be a sign unto you; Ye shall find the Babe wrapped in swaddling clothes, lying in a manger."

And immediately the sky was filled with a multitude of angels, praising and singing:

"Glory to God in the highest, and on earth peace, good will toward men."

When the angels disappeared, I was quickly ushered by my masters toward the City of David. I was nudged along by their staffs, but lambs are not easily hurried, so one of my masters picked me up and cradled me in his arms the rest of the way.

We had no trouble finding the place spoken of because the big star continued to rain down its light over the Baby. We found the Baby wrapped in swaddling clothes, with Mary and Joseph looking on. The swaddling clothes were another sign of where to find the Baby because we had been here before on another occasion. My masters knew exactly where to go from the signs. The Baby's name was Jesus, but we heard He was being called a King. He was God's Gift to the world.

We were in awe, and in reverence, I dropped to my knees and bowed my head. None of us had any worthy gifts to give a king. All we had was our love and adoration. The stable where Mary and Joseph were already staying, the feed trough where Jesus was lying, and the straw cushioning the inside of the trough were all loaned gifts to them because there was no other place in town for them to stay. Jesus seemed happy, though, with those simple gifts.

Meanwhile, hundreds of miles away in the East, three Magi (wise or educated men) had seen the star. These men were experts in the study of stars and were philosophers of noble birth and wealth. They also studied the prophecies foretelling of the Messiah's birth. Since they felt there was something very special about that big star, they decided to make the journey to see where it would lead them.

They followed it until it finally stopped over the house where Jesus was. It would have taken them months to make that journey, so by the time of their arrival, the little family would have moved to this house from the stable.

When the Magi arrived, they also knelt and offered Him gifts of gold, frankincense, and myrrh, as was their custom at the birth of royalty or rank.

Gold was a symbol of kingship and Jesus' deity. Frankincense was a perfume and a symbol of His purity. Myrrh was an embalming oil—a symbol of death.

But why was this a symbol of Jesus' death, since He had recently been born?

Jesus was also called the Lamb of God. In my family history, lambs without blemish or spot were sacrificed as offerings, usually at Passover. They were also used as a dedication offering of the first-born. We are a special flock, born in the Shepherd's Field between Bethlehem and Jerusalem, and set aside for Temple use.

In order to know if we can be set aside for this important duty, we are wrapped tightly in swaddling clothes and placed in a manger to calm us. Then our masters check us over for any blemishes, spots, bruises, scrapes, or broken bones. It is because of this symbolism and the star keeping watch that our masters knew exactly where to find Baby Jesus.

How interesting that we lambs not only represented Jesus at His birth in the manger, but also at his death as sacrificial lambs. Jesus was the Perfect Lamb! The prophecies said a Baby would be born who would later become *the Sacrificial Lamb* by dying on a cross.

Until that time, I am in line to become a sacrificial lamb, and this could become my big gift to Him. His gift would be His sacrifice for me, as the sacrificial offerings would no longer be needed after his death.

His sacrifice would also be a gift for you and the whole world, giving all an opportunity for eternity with our King, the Good Shepherd.

Thank you, Baby Jesus, for becoming the Shepherd of all our lives.

Resources

Ryrie Study Bible, Expanded Edition. King James Bible, 1986, 1994
Exodus 12:3-5
Leviticus 1:2, 3, 10
Numbers 24:17
Isaiah 9:2-6; 11:1-5; 49:1-11; 53:7
Micah 5:2
Matthew 2:1-15
Luke 2:1-38
John 1:29, 36
Peter 1:19

The Desire of Ages by Ellen G. White, Chapters 4, 5, and 6
The Mirror. "Sacrificial lambs and swaddling clothes," by Jenée Baldwin. Dec. 25. 2019, 11:13 a.m. (The Dawson Creek Mirror)
Ascension, "For the Last Days of Christmas: The Tower of the Flock" by Sonja Corbitt

Printed in the USA
CPSIA information can be obtained
at www.ICGtesting.com
LVHW072127100424
776970LV00016B/242